Autism:

Advancing on the Spectrum

From Inclusion
in School
to
Participation
in Life

Melissa Niemann
Danuta Highet

Foreword By
George Niemann, Ph. D.

PUBLISHED BY MAIDIN WORKS

This book is dedicated to Katherine.

Special thanks to George and Tom for their encouragement and to all who reviewed this book to help us make it better.

Foreword

Autism is a word familiar to many yet truly understood by few. Having spent over thirty-five years in the field, I have witnessed the growth of therapies and programs to support individuals with autism. For twenty of those years, I served as chief executive for a residential and day facility for over sixteen hundred children and adults with special needs, serving people in several states across the USA. Many of those served were on the spectrum of autism.

I mention my background to give you some perspective because in all these years, I have met thousands of families and professionals struggling with complex and sometimes insurmountable issues. Those years of service have allowed me to witness miraculous changes in people and appreciate what it takes to accomplish what many people think is impossible in a lifetime.

This book is based on experiences of inclusion efforts for a young woman, Katherine Highet, into the mainstream. In this, Katherine's true story, I have been privileged to see what happens when a mother and her family take on the indomitable spirit of faith, knowing that they will not rest until their daughter can function in society and enjoy life just like any of us. The family now wants to share the story of their struggle and successes with anyone else who is interested. This contributes to the greater good for others in similar situations. We are blessed to have this kind of dedication, given so selflessly by a courageous family.

What is the value or purpose, then, of writing this book? It is the gift of sharing what really inspires and keeps you going, despite incredible odds working against you – fighting the systems, skeptics and naysayers along the way while partnering with those who will help you succeed.

Katherine's many triumphs today have resulted from the efforts of a devoted family. As a united family unit, they would not accept institutionalization or marginalization and failure of their child to thrive; instead, they took charge of the challenges and directed the situations that they believed would allow their child the most fulfilling life possible. It goes far beyond scientific methodologies so popular today and emphasizes the importance of building human relationships in a social world. We are, after all, social creatures who need each other in vital ways. This story should inspire all of us. It illustrates in a simple, but poignant way, how you too can rise above tribulation by utilizing the power of perseverance, building stronger character and relying on faith and hope, which will not disappoint, as promised by our maker.

I can honestly say that, out of the thousands of families and people I have encountered in my "professional" as well as personal life, I have rarely been so moved by the invincible spirit possessed by Danuta Highet, Katherine's mother. It is that flame of indefatigability, optimism and love that burns within her that was, and continues to be, the catalyst for the changes that brought Katherine to a full life. We, the readers, are the privileged ones who can benefit so immensely from the lessons that Danuta and Melissa are willing to share with us. When professionals and families work together to accomplish a common goal, we can accomplish so much more.

So, let us learn from the lessons in this book and extend them. Most importantly, let's take their foundation of knowledge and experience to greater heights. Then remember to share our findings with others so we too can extend that circle of knowledge that we might discover along the way if we adopt the same principles of perseverance, tenacity and faith. It is a humbling but powerful experience. May you also be ready for the challenges ahead with renewed vigor!

George W. Niemann, Ph.D.

The intent of this book is to provide the reader with a quick overview of autism and encourage integration of a child with autism into school and community environments. Autism is not a static condition. A person with autism can learn and improve. Anyone can assist these individuals. This book will show you how every contact and interaction is a learning opportunity for a person on the autism spectrum. The better everyone understands this puzzling disorder, the more positive the impact on the individual. This book focuses on the school environment, but the lessons learned can be implemented anywhere in the community.

The information described, including the intervention techniques, is intended to inspire the reader. The material is not intended to be prescriptive nor does it replace any medical or professional advice. The consultation of a certified professional should be sought prior to implementing any behavioral plan.

Thank you for taking the time to read this book.

Everyone can make a difference!

Table of Contents

*It is our hope that this book will serve
to both guide and inspire you.*

*Whether your role is one of teacher, staff, peer or
parent, you can be part of a success story in the life
of a child. It is a challenge awaiting your action. You
can change the life of a child with autism not only for a
brief moment but forever.*

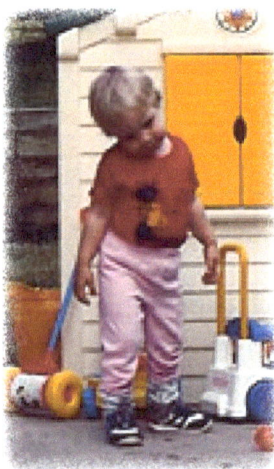

Introduction

The authors supported a young girl (Danuta's daughter Katherine) who is now a young woman, through inclusion settings from elementary school through middle school, high school, college and work experiences. As a result, her experiences were as rich as most typical children can possibly get. When she started inclusion in a regular education classroom, at 8 years old, her ability to maintain composure was less than 5 minutes. This duration gradually increased to several hours, then to full days. She was able to participate in after school activities such as chorus, community theater, dance school and color guard. Today she is able to participate in many activities and continues to learn. The information in this book is based on the experiences and lessons learned through Katherine's experience.

This is a unique guide written from the perspective of the educator and parent who supported her in school, during after school activities and now college. They would not be successful without the many individuals who participated in her inclusion. Teachers, students, community members and school administrative staff allowed flexibility in her programs.

Initially, many doubted that these efforts would succeed and a lot of convincing had to be done. Later it was Katherine who made everyone a believer. To see her grow from a person with autism predestined to live an isolated life, to a fun-loving, full participant in life who loves being with people, is a priceless reward.

Together, the authors have learned, through the use of best practices as well as trial and error, to help Katherine participate fully in school. Their goal was clear – to ensure positive learning experiences for the child with autism, her peers, and teachers. As Katherine progressed from elementary school through high school, new teams of teachers, peers, and staff were encountered. The authors discovered that the more information and training provided to the individuals surrounding the child, the better they interacted with her. The more teachers and peers were actively involved with the child, the more the child responded and participated in the activities. This became the formula for success.

Autism is a complex developmental disability that typically appears during the first three years of life. It is the result of a neurological disorder that affects the functioning of the brain. Autism knows no racial, ethnic, or social boundaries. Family income, life-style, and educational levels do not affect the chance of autism's occurrence. Autism interferes with the normal development of the brain primarily in the areas of social interaction and communication skills.

Children and adults with autism typically have difficulties in verbal and non-verbal communication, social interactions, and leisure or play activities. The disorder makes it hard for them to communicate with others and relate to the outside world. They may exhibit repeated body movements (hand flapping, rocking), unusual responses to people or attachments to objects, and they may resist changes in routines.

Over two million people in the U.S. today have some form of autism, which places it as the third most common developmental disability—more than five times more common than Down Syndrome. Yet most of the public, including many professionals in the medical, educational, and vocational fields, are still unaware of how autism affects people and how to effectively work with individuals with autism.

Who is affected?

Autism Spectrum Disorders (ASD) occur in all racial, ethnic, and

socioeconomic groups, but are four times more likely to occur in boys than in girls. The Centers for Disease Control (CDC) estimates that between

1 in 110 children in the United States have an ASD.

What are autism spectrum disorders?

Autism spectrum disorders (ASDs) are a group of developmental anomalies in the brain. Scientists do not know yet exactly what causes ASDs. ASDs can impact a person's functioning at different levels, from very mild to severe. There is usually nothing about how a person with an ASD looks that sets him apart from other people, but he may communicate, interact, behave, and learn in ways that are different from most people. Thinking and learning abilities of people with ASDs can vary – from gifted to severely challenged. Autistic disorder is the most commonly known type of ASD, but there are others, including "pervasive developmental disorder-not otherwise specified" (PDD-NOS) and Asperger Syndrome.

What are some of the signs of ASDs?

People with ASDs may have problems with social, emotional, and communication skills. They might repeat certain behaviors and might not want change in their daily activities. Many people with ASDs also have different ways of learning, paying attention, or reacting to stimuli. ASDs begin during early childhood and last throughout a person's life.

> An average of
> # 1 in 110
> children in the United States have an ASD.

A child or an adult with an ASD might:

- not relate to others or not have an interest in other people at all, avoid eye contact, or want to be alone

- not play "pretend" games, (feeding a doll)

- not point to show interest, (an airplane flying overhead)

- not look at objects when another person points at them

- have trouble understanding other people's feelings or expressing their own emotions

- prefer not to be held or cuddled or might cuddle only when they want to

- appear to be unaware when other people talk to them but respond to other sounds

- be very interested in people, but not know how to talk, play, or relate to them

- parrot words or phrases (echolalia)

- have trouble expressing their needs using typical words or gestures

- repeat actions over and over again (spnning objects)

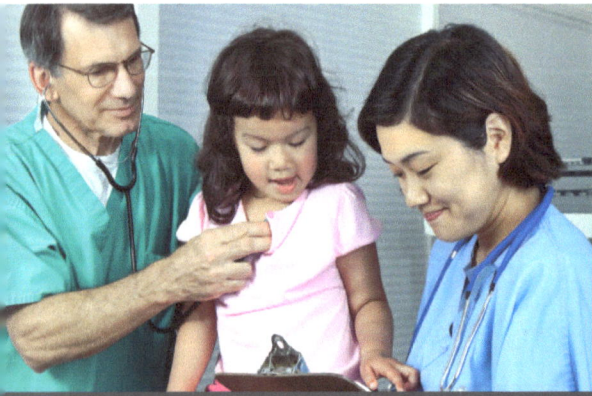

- have trouble adapting when a routine changes

- have unusual sensory reactions to the way things smell, taste, look, feel, or sound

- repeat same "script" or song over and over again

- lose skills they once had (stop saying words or stop smiling)

- line things up repeatedly

What can I do if I think my child has an ASD?

Talk with your child's doctor. If you or your doctor think there could be a problem, ask for a referral to see a pediatric neurologist or other specialist. Otherwise you can contact your local early intervention agency (for children under 3) or public school (for children 3 and older).

To find out who to speak to in your area, you can contact the National Information Center for Children and Youth with Disabilities (NICHCY) by logging onto www.nichcy.org or calling 1-800-695-0285. In addition, the Centers for Disease Control and Prevention (CDC) have links to information for families on their Autism Information Center Web page at www. cdc.gov/ncbdd/dd/aic/resources. (See Other Resources section, page 67).

18

Autism - A Personal Perspective

Autism is a disorder that is more common than Down Syndrome, yet the general public is often not familiar with it. Most people are familiar with the movie "Rain Man," which depicts a savant with autism. There are less than 20 savants with autism in the world today; therefore, the image depicted in "Rain Man" represents a fraction of a percent of all the individuals with autism.

The degree of severity of autism varies within each individual. Depending on the senses affected by the disorder and the ability to process different types of information, the severity of symptoms and behaviors will vary. As the authors have discovered, the abilities will change over time due to intervention and/or treatment. Therefore, the needs of an individual will constantly change.

Some individuals with autism are nonverbal, while others speak fluently but don't understand all the social implications of our language.

An individual's lack of ability to fully understand and communicate generates frustration. This becomes more apparent whenever demands are placed on the person with autism or when they can't communicate their needs. This frustration is usually exhibited in behaviors that are abnormal and disruptive.

Another characteristic that individuals with autism exhibit is stimulatory behavior. These behaviors help them deal with a daily routine and help them shut out the outside world. It appears that our brain is starved for input just as our bodies need food. When this input is cut off by the environment, the behaviors help deliver this constant need for input. Everyone exhibits some of the behaviors in this category, to a lesser degree, during a time of boredom or inactivity.

> There are less than 20 savants with autism in the world today.

19

For example, self-stimulatory behaviors can be observed when people are in a traffic jam (tapping to music, nail biting, etc.), or waiting in a long line.

The lack of awareness affects another important aspect of a person with autism, her safety.

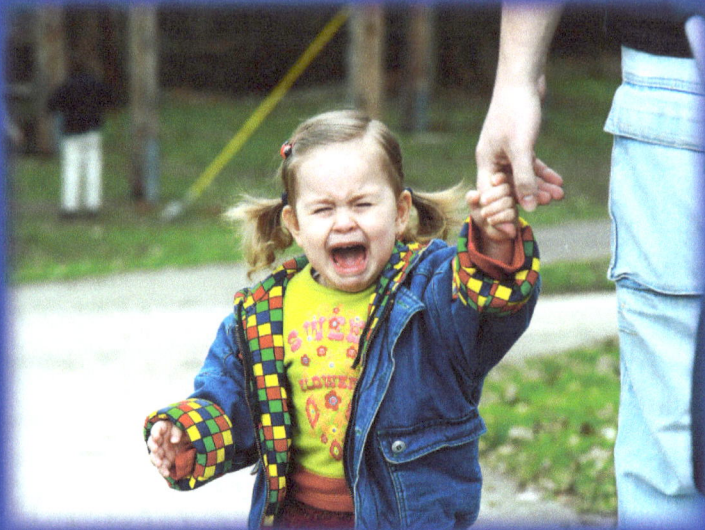

Children with autism may rock, self talk, or spin objects.

These behaviors cause further isolation of the individuals with autism. Parents, when unable to control a child in public, often deal with constant embarrassment and disapproval. They may feel they have to protect their child and their own emotions from the uninformed general public. This will further isolate the person with autism from the learning opportunities that our community has to offer.

The child's inability to understand the dangers of the surroundings poses constant risk, such as consumption of inedibles, running out into the street, or lack of recognition of common dangers. This puts constant pressure on the child's caretakers to monitor her at all times. Having a child with autism may result in the isolation of the whole family unit.

Behavioral and communication issues keep individuals with autism from interacting in the community.

A caretaker, in a public area with a young screaming child will receive looks of disapproval. Many "helpful" bystanders might offer advice, point, or whisper as to the capabilities of the caretaker. Many behaviors will not be tolerated in stores, restaurants, or theaters. As a result, a child with autism may not have opportunities to interact and will withdraw further. The downward spiral effect of this without intervention will result in total isolation.

The majority of individuals with autism do not have physical disabilities or different physical features. They can learn and grow as any other person. However, they must be taught in a way that will allow learning to occur. This involves specialized techniques and methods, which must be practiced until attention and absorption of information are achieved.

As everyone grows and explores the world, they are constantly learning. A person with autism misses those learning opportunities when they shut out experiences.

> **"Helpful" bystanders will offer advice, point, or whisper.**

There is no magic pill that can reverse the long-term effects of autism. At this point in time, any hope that the individuals with autism might have for a normalized life requires a tremendous group effort of intervention. This means the parents, teachers, peers, staff and community must work together to help each and every individual with autism.

> **Autism is a disorder in which one person's efforts can make a tremendous difference.**

21

When those efforts are multiplied, miracles can happen. Those who are reading this book are becoming part of a solution for autism. They may not be able to pull the individual out alone, but together they may be able to reach in and save the person with autism from a life of isolation.

For every child, the daily routine is a world of discovery filled with learning opportunities. A child with autism is not different in this aspect, he needs to be learning as well. The creation of these learning opportunities and learning how to teach the child with autism is what we all need to master.

Sometimes when they are learning, children with autism retreat for protection from excessive sensory inputs. Try to identify any external causes for the regression or changes that may have had this effect.

Teaching a child with autism can feel like a roller coaster ride. Make sure you and the child enjoy the ride as much as possible despite the ups and downs.

DO NOT GIVE UP

WHEN YOUR CHILD SUDDENLY REGRESSES OR APPEARS TO LOSE THE SKILLS YOU TAUGHT.

As the authors have discovered, the diagnosis of autism does not need to be a static condition. A person with autism can learn. As he learns, he progresses on the spectrum. Improved communication and social skills replace the need for tantrums. As self stimulatory behaviors are replaced with more appropriate stimulatory behaviors, the person gains more self control. That, in turn, allows him to interact more easily with others. The more he interacts, the more he will be approached. It's an ongoing cycle, where the frequency of interactions continue to increase. This leads to an increased interest in the world around him.

Imagine that you are traveling abroad, cannot speak the language, and have a migraine headache. Bright lights are shining in your eyes. You would probably use body language to try and explain your condition. If others did not understand your body language and continued to place demands on you, what would you do? You might run, scream or kick. That is how a person with autism might react when demands are placed on him. An individual with autism may not be able to express if he has a headache or toothache. He may be sensitive to loud noises, or smells. Instead of communicating his needs, he may resort to disruptive behavior to express that something is wrong.

Disruptive Behaviors

Communication and Social Skills

The chart above shows how a person with autism can advance on the spectrum. The difficulty is in recognizing where the child is on the spectrum, then acquiring the knowledge and skills you need to help him move to the next level. Get the disruptive behaviors under control first and communication skills will improve, allowing you to move on the spectrum.

As language and comprehension of what's going on around them increases, they have an opportunity to express their fear, pain and other emotions using words instead of behaviors. When they learn to understand their own emotions and feelings, they are then ready to learn and understand the emotions of others.

A typical chart of a child with autism will show scattered skills compared to a typically developing child. The 7 year old child may have the skill level of a 6 month old in language development, the fine motor skills may be at a 16 month developmental level, yet gross motor skills may be age appropriate or older. Each skill is a building block of its own. As you expand each skill, the child progresses on the spectrum. Some skills are interdependent and you may observe progress slowing down.

Don't get discouraged.

Don't get discouraged. Try and identify what's slowing you down. Focus working on another skill. The most important aspect is to keep teaching new skills and combining them so generalization to other skills can be maximized. See the section "Learning Differences" (page 40).

Typical progression of skill building:

Type of prompt	Full Prompt	Partial	Faded
Physical Most Restrictive	-hand-over-hand method -physically turning or placing -moving arms or legs -forming lips through the motion of sounds or words You actually perform a task together. You move her hand or foot or whole body to guide her to understand what she needs her body to do to perform the task.	With success you fade the physical contact to a less restrictive prompt. You may start a turn but let her finish.	Keep reducing the amount of grip or touch until it's no longer there and a verbal or visual cue alone can be used.
Verbal Less Restrictive	When you actually say what you want her to do or ask her to repeat what you've modeled. "Turn around" "Banana." Say: "My name is Katherine."	As soon as the child is successful with full prompt start reducing the prompt gradually: "Turn ah" "bana", "ba" Say :"My name is Ka" Say: "My name is"	Keep reducing the verbal prompt until she can independently say it. "Turn" "b" "My" Answer "What is your name?" independently.
Visual Least Restrictive	You use gestures to prompt the person to perform an action. The advantage of visual prompting is that it can be done at a distance from the person. It also makes the person become more aware of her surroundings.	Stand close by and use the gesture. Gradually move farther and farther away.	You may be able to prompt from across the room by using a facial expression, pointing, or a discrete sign that she understands. You may be able to point to a peer that is behaving appropriately to model the expectations.

Any skill can be taught using this method. You will pair the physical and verbal at first and then keep fading as the child progresses.

The most important aspect is to reward each attempt and vary the rewards for greatest impact. Save the best rewards for the best attempts. Rewards need to be immediate. Promises of going on the swings later are useless. As soon as you get a great response go and swing!

Skill Progression

All skills may need to progress in this way. As the child learns "how to learn", the new skills may be started at higher levels. Initially, the simple skills may take months to teach. But as the child moves along the spectrum, the skills will take less time to teach and you will be able to start teaching him at higher and higher levels.

ONE-ON-ONE LEARNING: DIRECT TEACHING

One-on-One

1 The child is taught the skill in a quiet environment away from any other distractions. Goal: child performs the task independently and follows simple commands.

Skill Generalization Across Materials

2 The skills need to be generalized. Just because the child learned to look at a photo of a bird does not mean that the child actually knows that it's a bird. It could be that the card you used has a bend in it and he knows that when he sees that card he needs to say "bird".

Skill Generalization Across People

3 Just because the skill is performed for one person does not mean that the skill is acquired. We prompt without meaning to at times. You may squint or twitch unknowingly. The child may be focused on you, not the target materials, to give the correct response.

26

Skill Generalization in the Community

4 The same skill is now taken outside of the work/therapy room and may require many more attempts or prompt/fading with each new environment. Depending on the environment, the noises or sensory overload may interfere with the child's attending abilities.

When the student does pick up others' behaviors, you have succeeded!

SMALL GROUP LEARNING: INDIRECT TEACHING

Peer Modeling

1 Once a child can observe what you do and is able to imitate, bring in a peer, and teach the child to observe and imitate the peer. By watching a peer, the child is able to figure out what to do. You may be concerned that the child will pick up other inappropriate behaviors from the peer. Most behaviors have a functional purpose that serve the individual with autism. When the child does pickup others' behaviors, you have succeeded! Now move to teach what are appropriate or inappropriate behaviors.

Small groups

2 Increase the number of peers until he is able to learn in a small group and he has the ability to follow multistep directions. Natural environments are best for generalization and optimal learning.

CLASSROOM LEARNING

Introduction

1 The child can remain in a classroom without disturbing other students. This may take multiple trials in short intervals increasing over time.

Classroom Work

2 The student is able to work in a classroom environment on skills that were previously mastered in a one-on-one therapy environment.

Classroom Skills

3 The student is able to learn to work in a classroom environment on class materials along with other students. He learns to follow class routine; taking notes, quizzes, or handing in homework. Once a single class is "mastered" the student can expand to other classes such as music or art. Some classes may be easier to start with than others.

Physical education class may be good for one student as a first class, but math class may be the best place to start for another. The more structured the classroom, the sooner the student will be able to understand what is expected of him.

School Skills

4 Once the student is able to learn in a classroom environment, the transitioning from class to class, or activity to activity, is an important next level skill. Learning how to act in a cafeteria, or the library, helps the student acquire skills that will be important in the community. Following schedules and having schedules disrupted is part of life. An individual with autism needs to learn these skills just like any other student.

Participation in Community and After School Activities

5 Generalizing school skills to life skills is a great way of helping to ensure that the child will have a rich and fulfilling future. The same process can be used to teach the student to participate in any activity. Using a similar step by step approach, generalize these skills to a movie theater or a place of worship. Cafeteria skills can be taken to a restaurant, family gathering or a party.

INDIVIDUAL LEARNING:

Homework

1 The student needs to learn how to complete his homework assignments. Initially a lot of prompting and modeling may be required. Simply getting through the process is reinforcing.

Studying for Tests

2 As any other activity the student with autism may need to learn how to learn independently. She will need to learn how to study, memorize, and research information. This is not just a school type of activity. This will enable the student to continue to learn without being told to do so.

Our lives are constantly changing. Technology is changing careers and opportunities. For an individual with autism "to learn how to learn" may be the most important life skill you will teach.

Life is Noisy and Messy!

28

Always try to teach one step above where you think the child's current level is. When starting a new skill you may need to go back to one-on-one teaching and then move to a less restrictive method. This will give the individual an opportunity to succeed at the higher level.

POSITIVE REINFORCEMENT! Use it! Vary it! It Works!

As you are teaching more and more complex skills, you may need to return a full prompt or hand over hand method. Don't get discouraged. It's not you or the child. It's often the complexity of the information that you are teaching. A typical child understands abstract concepts naturally through learning and observation...

BREAKING DOWN SKILLS:

Every skill can be broken down to smaller components. Using a method called "backward chaining" can give the child a feel of instant accomplishment. Usually it is most rewarding. For example:

Making a Sandwich
1. Take out plate
2. Take out bread
3. Take out knife
4. Take out jelly
5. Open jelly
6. Use knife to get jelly
7. Spread jelly on bread
8. Eat bread and jelly

Start with step 7 and 8, and then move to 6,7,8 and so on.

Writing a Word
You write "ca" and partial "t" without the dash, and child completes the word. Say, " You wrote cat!" and give lots of rewards! Once he can do this, you can write "ca", then "c", and than just the command "Write cat." and he writes the word "cat".

Teaching in "chunks"
Teach each step separately and gradually put them together.

One of the most likely reasons a student with autism may not function successfully in the mainstream population is the behavior that she may exhibit. The strange, somewhat bizarre "stimming" behaviors are difficult for most to ignore. They make the individual with autism appear irrational and therefore somewhat threatening. Most individuals with autism attend specialized schools.

Some behaviors may appear "cute" when a child is young. You need to imagine a 200 pound man or woman doing this same behavior in an office environment. Is it still "cute"? Most likely not. You need to eradicate this behavior. The longer the behavior is performed, the harder it will be for you to replace it or extinguish it.

Getting these **behaviors under control** is the number one priority for a student with autism. Finding ways for her to "stim" in a socially acceptable manner may be one way to combat this difficult task.

The child can learn to control the stimulatory behaviors or replace them with other more acceptable behaviors. The authors have found that the longer the child is required to control these behaviors, the easier it is for her to do so. Consequently, self-control becomes a practiced, positive behavior.

The environment needed to mainstream an individual with autism is a well-organized classroom. Communications are clear and consistent, and the teacher maintains a well disciplined and controlled environment. You may have been selected as a teacher for a student with autism because of your comprehensive teaching style and organizational skills.

The student's success in the classroom environment can depend on you and your management style.

Providing structure helps communicate expectations to the student with autism. When she can follow a routine, she is able to understand what activities are next, how long each activity takes and all the other things we take for granted. She is able to relax in this type of environment and flourish.

with autism reaches school age, her peer group spends most of the day at school and in after school activities.

School hours maximize opportunities for socialization and cannot afford to be "lost time" for the student with autism. Starting with small, simple steps, such as greetings, the child with autism must learn a hierarchy of social skills already second nature to most of her peers.

Academic achievement may be of secondary importance to the building of behavioral and social skills.

As children succeed in this environment, you may want to start teaching in a less controlled environment. Let's face it, the world around us is chaotic. She needs to learn how to focus in an unstructured environment.

Learning social skills is often very difficult for a child with autism. Therefore, peers are critical role models. By the time the child

Academic skills can be taught one on one outside of school, but the social and behavioral skills must be taught in a mainstream environment where the person with autism must learn to function. Remember, a child can learn to read and write and compute, but ultimately she must use these skills in a meaningful way. Social, behavioral, and communication practices bridge this gap.

31

The most simple task of sitting quietly for an hour of class time may take a year to acquire. Once the child can accomplish this simple task, a new world will open up for her. Now she may be able to attend a movie, a religious service, a wedding, play, or a dinner with the family at a restaurant, a family gathering, a club meeting, a concert... and new opportunities abound that were not previously available.

Some behaviors may be amusing when a child is performing it. Imagine an adult doing the same behavior.

are, when you are teaching the child to coexist in a regular classroom setting, the child with autism will need to sit up straight while other students are slouching. This is because the other students can straighten up independently when a situation arises. The children with autism need to practice the best behavior at all times to learn the norm.

The skills she acquires in the classroom will help her succeed into adulthood. The people in a work environment are generally not as knowledgeable or as understanding as those in a school environment.

When aiming for appropriate behavior in a classroom, you must aim higher than you would for typical children. Their manners and posture need to be better than their peers. Chances Many adults with autism are unable to maintain employment due to the behavioral issues and not their capability to meet the job requirements.

Your success in dealing with these behaviors may help assure a successful, independent life for a person with autism.

The prospect of future employment opportunities will diminish with a tantrum or inappropriate behavior. Once the children with autism become adults, their peers will be working. To be with people their age, they need to behave in a nonthreatening manner. Expectations must be reasonable but attainable.

Behavior as a Communication Tool

When any individual gets upset or frustrated, communication does not come as easily. Emotion takes over logic. People often use behavior to try and change a situation. An outraged person may slam things, raise his voice, scream or run out because he is unable to verbally express himself or he may feel like no one is listening. Some individuals with autism never get beyond this level of communication. Therefore, when a child with autism is "misbehaving", you need to analyze the reason for the behavior, since the child will not be able to verbalize his fears and dislikes.

When typical individuals are alone, they listen to a radio or music or talk to themselves. The brain requires constant stimulation. The input to the brain is as necessary as food or water is to human survival. Stimulatory input helps individuals deal with anger, frustration, or boredom. For example, when music is piped into elevators, it helps people deal easier with a crowded or claustrophobic environment. For instance, a wave is created during a sports event, an activity that helps spectators cope with unoccupied time.

Since many individuals with autism shut off the input from outside, they become very skillful in generating their own self-stimulatory behavior in order to calm and satisfy their brain. These stimulatory behaviors help them deal with a situation, and they use the behaviors to regulate themselves.

These behaviors might also shut out external information, which means that opportunities for learning are lost. As a result, the child with autism does not pick up the skills that typical peers assimilate by participating and interacting with the environment.

An individual with autism can exhibit a wide variety of behaviors. Frustration or lack of understanding of what is expected can result in a behavior that is erratic, aggressive

or startling in nature. By the time a child with autism is in a classroom in a public school, he learns to control these behaviors. They are the first to be brought under control, so that they do not interfere with the individual's learning, or the instruction of other students in the classroom.

Behaviors do not occur without a cause. There is always a reason for the behavior being exhibited. Behavior is the most primitive communication tool that people fall back on when they cannot use language to communicate.

Here are some examples of behaviors and possible messages that the child may be conveying:

Behavior	Possible Message
Crying, pushing, biting nails, squeezing an arm or pinching	- This is too difficult. - I am tired. - I want something but I don't know how to ask for it. - I don't like this. - I am afraid. - This hurts me. - I don't want to do this.
Kicking, throwing objects, pulling hair, screaming	I tried to tell someone before but they do not listen to me until I react in a physical manner. Wow, this was effective. Next time I will try that or something even louder!
Posing, facial grimaces	- I am pretending to be a character in my own scene. - I am nervous and involuntary ticks take over. - I am sensitive to your smell.
Humming, singing, self talk, covering ears, reciting parts of movies	- I do not like the noise or it's too loud. - I am bored and I am occupying myself. - I am shutting you out so that I can hear my own noises better. - I like the tune in my head.
Rocking, shaking leg, erratic movements, spinning self, spinning objects, flapping hands, flicking fingers	- Body has to do something because the brain commands it to stay occupied. - It is fun, like dancing, I like how this feels. - If I do this they leave me alone. - If I do this that gets their attention.
Laugh out-loud	- I just thought of something funny. - I think this is funny.
Eating inedibles (paper, glass, trash)	- I need to feel this texture or flavor. - I am bored. - I may have a vitamin deficiency or other medical condition.
Collecting of information such as phone numbers, car types, names, addresses, telling the same story over and over again	- I want to talk with you but I don't know how to converse. - The world is confusing but I will put you in a category or a list so I know where you fit. - I like the way this sounds over and over again.

In extreme cases, some of the behaviors may be self-mutilating (pulling out own hair, eye gauging, biting self, head banging.) The reasons may be any of the above. Handling these types of behaviors requires monitoring and specialized training.

Lack of social awareness will also cause a child with autism to exhibit socially unacceptable behavior at times. Often, they do not understand that behaviors such as nose picking are not appropriate. This lack of awareness is due to their earlier inability to pick up social cues naturally from parents or peers.

These are important behaviors to address since they will likely result in avoidance by other children and future co-workers. You will need to prioritize the behaviors on which you focus. There may be a different set of behaviors you are working on depending on what environment you occupy.

For example, sitting without disturbing others may be one of the first behaviors you focus on in a math class. The cafeteria may present a great opportunity to work on standing in line without touching others, saying thank you, saying hello and goodbye.

Behavior Life Cycle

Those interacting with the individual can affect how the person interacts in the environment. There are behaviors that need to be eliminated or replaced with more appropriate ones. Other behaviors, namely language and social interactions, need to be increased. The behavior life cycle is as follows:

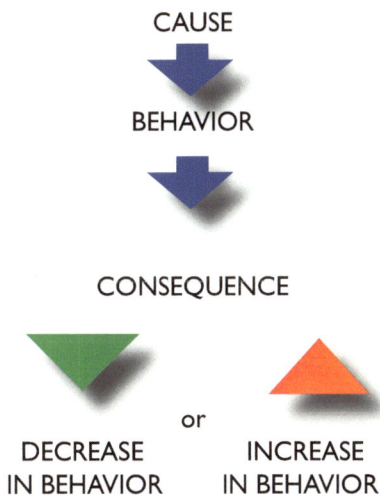

CAUSE

BEHAVIOR

CONSEQUENCE

DECREASE   or   INCREASE
IN BEHAVIOR   IN BEHAVIOR

When you observe a negative behavior, you need to evaluate the reason for this behavior in order to help eliminate it, decrease it, or replace it.

The easiest way to eliminate the bad behavior is to eliminate the cause. If you cannot eliminate the cause, the second best way to control it is by consequence.

Example A
A child is screaming because he wants a toy:

Consequence 1
Give up and give the child the toy (this consequence will increase the behavior and next time the child will scream even louder and longer).

Consequence 2
Remove the child from the classroom until the child stops screaming. He can come back to play when quiet.

Example B
A child is screaming because he does not want to perform the assignment:

Consequence 1
Removing the child from the classroom for a time-out will most likely increase the bad behavior. He escapes the task.

Consequence 2
Remove the child from the classroom and work on the task outside of the classroom, making the task more difficult.

Quite often we tend to focus on the bad behavior and inadvertently we reinforce and increase it. Giving the attention to good behavior will increase it. This is true for the typical peers as well. If you'd like to increase the initiations from the peers towards the child with autism, you need to reward him at every instant.

For example, " That was great how you helped John sit up straight." This is specific verbal feedback.

There are effective ways to increase good behaviors, such as initiations or good eye contact. The consequences can be used to increase the good behaviors.

Your Action	
Ignoring the behavior	Not giving acknowledgement that anything occurred.
	This will at times make behaviors disappear without any intervention, especially if combined with a replacement behavior. Providing alternative ways to communicate, increasing language, and teaching appropriate behaviors will often reduce undesirable behaviors.
Focusing on the bad behavior	Using punishment, reprimand, loss of privileges.
	This backfires a lot of the time and may result in an increase in that behavior especially if the cause of it is attention seeking. We use this because it provides quicker results immediately, but these results are not long lasting.
Focusing on the absence of the bad behavior	Using positive reinforcement, rewards, and verbal praise when the bad behavior is missing, for example, person is not flapping his hands. ("You're sitting so nicely.")
Focusing on good behavior	Using positive reinforcement, rewards, and verbal praise.
	IT WORKS!!! In the long run, by giving positive feedback, you indirectly communicate to the child that this is what you want him to do.
Replacing behavior	Self-stimulatory behaviors are usually not eliminated but replaced with a higher-level stimulatory behavior, which is socially acceptable. For example: reading, listening to music, watching TV, crafts, playing games, solitaires, etc, provide the brain with a constant supply of information to keep it occupied.

Your first reaction might be to punish a child for "misbehaving". By doing this, you may be taking away the only tool the child with autism has to communicate, which could force him into further withdrawal. This makes it a challenge to constantly evaluate the situation to determine what the child with autism is trying to communicate behaviorally.

There may be a situation where "negative" reinforcement is required. If you use punishment or reprimands you need to monitor whether the behavior is increasing as a result of intervention or consequence. The first step is to try to use alternative strategies. As an adult present in these situations, you may face your own emotional responses to these behaviors.

You may feel embarrassment for the child with autism, in front of other children or other adults. It is critical to deal with the situation in a controlled manner so that the "damage" is minimized and the individual is corrected in a way that he can learn. You will need to focus on the consequence and put your emotion and feelings aside.

Mainstream peers can be taught by example. You can demonstrate how a situation with a child with autism can be handled in a positive and productive manner. As a result, you will teach the other children how to help a child with autism learn these important skills.

Positive reinforcement works on typical children as well. You may increase peer interactions by providing plenty of positive reinforcement for those peers that initiate an interaction or assistance to the child with autism.

Learning Differences

The development of an individual with autism differs from normal individuals. Frequently, communication skills and language will be lagging. Social skills are always affected in the individual with autism due to the nature of the disorder. Fine and

gross motor skills may or may not be affected. However, each child with autism has different skills and abilities.

It is difficult to develop one single technique to help all children with autism. Nevertheless, specific behavioral techniques have been proven to be most effective. Each child with autism requires a tailored approach to develop the most effective way for him to learn.

Just as the teacher uses auditory, visual and hands-on materials to teach typical children, a person teaching a child with autism will use different approaches. A teacher may be able to explain tasks verbally to mainstream students, and they will be able to understand. The same technique used with a child with autism may show no results.

Most children learn 16 hours a day; a child with autism has to work very hard to acquire a fraction of the skills of their peers. As the child acquires skills, the teaching methods must be changed to transition from a one-on-one environment to a group environment. To teach intricate social skills, the child with autism must be surrounded by peer models to observe these skills. It becomes more difficult

to create this type of an environment 16 hours per day as the child gets older. The language and skills become more abstract and peers find it more reinforcing to interact on a higher intellectual level.

Methods of intervention vary according to the needs and age of the child with autism. Because most children with autism must first learn how to attend to a task, strict and specific techniques are used early on to teach attention. One of these methods is discrete trial, which teaches skills in very small increments. Once attention is learned and compliance assured, information is presented in its simplest form and practiced in a one-on-one environment until mastery is complete.

This method of teaching is one part of a larger treatment model called ABA or Applied Behavior Analysis. While the individual with autism is learning, his behaviors are continuously analyzed to determine what needs

must be addressed. This close monitoring allows the parents, the

Typically, we learn 16 hours a day.

child and therapists to participate in an intensive, structured program specific to the needs of each child.

As he learns more and more skills, it takes less and less effort to teach him...as a result he is taught how to learn.

Physical Prompting

If children do not attend to a task, they may be able to learn by being physically prompted through the task. It may take many trials to actually teach the task. The point is that they can learn. The difficulty is figuring out

the best way to teach each task. This may be the first step required before any learning takes place. You perform this method by using prompting and fading techniques. A hand-over-hand method may be used at first, where you may hold the child's hand and perform the task together. Slowly the grip is faded until it can be totally removed and the child can perform the skill independently. The teacher, therapist, or parent will physically move the child's hands, arms or whole body in order for her to experience the motion of performing the task.

The challenge is to be creative and persistent in your trials because it may take hundreds of trials to teach a very simple task. As the child gets the idea and starts to perform the task, the grip gets lighter and lighter until he performs the task independently.

Learning to imitate

Next, the child learns to imitate by learning to observe a person and mimicking the gesture. A simple command "Do this!" is taught and the child can now learn many new tasks. This technique is taught in a one-on-one environment. **Many fine motor and gross motor skills can be taught once the child understands this simple command.** These skills can then be generalized to other environments.

Modeling

The expression "a picture is worth a thousand words" is even truer for an individual with autism. If you can explain the task visually, it may make it easier for a child to understand than a detailed verbal description. Once the child can imitate, he can learn a skill or language being modeled by others. This continues until the child can learn by observing others independently.

Observing others is very difficult for children with autism. Many individuals with autism avoid eye contact. This particularly interferes with the learning of language and communication. Observing facial expressions and body language are critical components of communication. Nonverbal communication is also a critical skill which can be learned by modeling or "posture" prompts.

Learning Language

A child with autism will most likely be very delayed in language and communication. Learning language is a complex and time sensitive process. It involves the building of vocabulary, syntax, morphology and grammar through repetition of auditory and visual cues over a long period of time. **A child with autism may have one or more of these avenues blocked.**

Once the child can imitate, the skills can be built up. Sounds are built up to words, words to phrases, phrases to sentences, etc. Initially, each sentence may be taught rote, then they are prompted to the child. Slowly prompts are faded until the child is able to initiate them independently.

Receptive (understood) language is usually a precursor to the expressive language. However, **if the child learns the expressive (word) part first, it can then become understood or meaningful when put in context.**

43

Learning Communication

Although the student may be able to speak sentences, there are many aspects of communication that cannot be easily taught in a one-on-one environment. As individuals get older, the understanding of emotions, can say to one person but not to another. Similarly, there are physical gestures and facial expressions that may change the context of what's being communicated. Discrimination can be critical. Imagine speaking to a police officer in the same way you speak to a friend!

There are no classes devoted to this concept. Everyone learns these concepts naturally by interacting with their environment. In our society, communication is the basis for socialization; relationships, and multiple meanings becomes more and more abstract. Words have multiple meanings as well as situational meanings. For example, a tone of voice may imply a different message. These are the finer nuances of language. Imagine the different meanings "No way!" might be expressed in different tones of voice.

There are manners and socially acceptable comments someone therefore, **if children with autism cannot learn how to communicate, their social lives will be very limited.**

A typical child learns social skills throughout the day as she interacts with others and her environment. Many resources and much effort are required to teach these skills to an individual with autism. It may not be as rewarding personally for someone to carry on a conversation about a very simplified topic. The reader needs to keep in mind that to the child with autism, it may be as difficult to converse as for the average person to talk about nuclear physics. Just keep him talking!

Learning to Perform Tasks

Other skills are taught in a similar manner as language: a dot is expanded to a line, a line to a letter, letter to a word, etc. More complex tasks may need to be broken into smaller tasks, which are later combined. Tasks may be taught by a method called backward chaining, where the task is broken down and taught from the last sequence forward.

Tasks may be presented at a slower speed with fewer steps while the speed and complexity will be gradually increased until the task can be performed.

Generalization

A unique characteristic of individuals with autism is that although they may learn a task in one environment, they may not automatically carry it out in another.

Therefore, the same method may need to be repeated in many environments before the child generalizes a skill. For example, a child may learn to ask a question but might not ask the question of anyone else or in a different environment. She may learn how to tie a ribbon but might not be able to tie her shoes.

Another aspect of generalization is that the individual may learn a skill in the quiet environment of a therapy room; however, if she leaves the room she may not be able to perform any of these skills due to distractions such as

noise, odors, lights, etc. The skills may need to be retaught in an environment filled with distractions.

Although these methods are initially used to teach the child with autism, they are useful, as well, to teach more complicated and abstract information later. Generalization is the key to successful skill building. If the skill is established across environments, it is less likely to be lost than those learned in isolation.

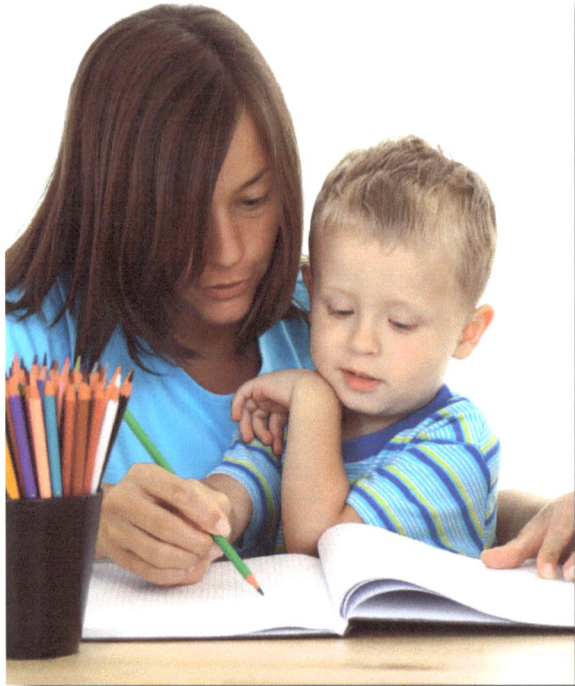

Inclusion in a Regular Education Class

Much preparation is needed prior to bringing a student into the classroom. You need to make everyone aware of what is to happen. Giving them a copy of this book may help them understand why you are doing this. This may include staff, teachers, students, cafeteria staff, etc. You will want to do this without the student present or before the student arrives, so that every one can freely ask you questions about the student.

You may want to tell peers what the student is like, including personal interests. For example, does she like dogs, what are her favorite movies, foods, games, etc.? Make everyone aware of how you may need to interact with her. Let everyone know how they can help. They will need to understand that the student may need to be removed out of the classroom or school, and why this is happening.

Select the seat in the classroom possibly in the back of the class, so the student can observe other students, and preferably closest to the door, so you can quickly exit without disturbing anyone.

Limit the stay in the classroom to what you think the student can handle without disturbing others. **If 5 minutes is all she can do, that's fine for starters.**

Use Positive Reinforcement with Student, Teachers and Peers.

It's not necessary for the student to be able to do the work that the class is doing in order to work on appropriate classroom behaviors. She needs to feel successful, so the worksheets she is working on may need to be mastered in a one-on-one environment, first. Then you can generalize these worksheets to the classroom. Constantly reward the behavior you are working on. Gradually increase the time in the classroom, for longer and longer periods without disturbing other students.

As you progress with being able to behave properly in a classroom you move to the next goals:

* greetings
* taking notes
* getting supplies
* taking tests

- raising hand and answering questions (simplified question at first that is mastered in one-on-one) or working with the teacher as a partner is a great way to get this accomplished
- becoming friends with other students (you need to be-friend students first, since initial interactions between the student and their peers will be through you and your prompted responses)
- working on class work, etc.

The same strategies for bringing a student into a classroom can be used for other activities or for an adult with autism that is starting a new job.

Inclusion in an Activity

The same guidelines that are used to include an individual in a classroom would apply for an activity. The only difference is the preparation. You need to go and observe the activity first. Look at what skills are needed to perform the activity. You need to pre teach some of these skills in a one-on-one environment.

After each session you may continue to teach the skills in a one-on-one environment. Other members of the activity may advance by what they learn during the activity. The individual with autism may need more trials to accomplish the same thing. Incremental learning is important in an inclusion activity. Not everything can be mastered at once. Start teaching a skill at a slower rate and gradually speed up as the task gets easier.

A lot of organizers that work at after school activities will not have the same teaching skills or background as the regular school staff. You may be fully responsible for all the teaching and rewarding of the individual with autism. You will need to give lots of positive feedback to the staff and other participants.

Chances are that you will not have the same resources available as during the school day.

These activities are usually in a more chaotic environment.

Less structure may be more confusing, and there may be more unexpected or sudden noises or other distractions. The facility may be loud or filled with lots of noisy kids.

You may start in small steps:

- allow five minutes for sitting in the new environment
- increase duration of proper behavior

- work on the skills at a successful level, next to the peers
- ask for volunteers to practice a new skill on the side

- prompt fully at first
- provide lots of rewards for the child with autism
- reward students who volunteer, make them feel special
- thank those in charge of the activity, asking them for feedback (their input can be invaluable)
- try new things, if they work, continue; if not, brainstorm with others for ideas and creative solutions

Selecting activities that are right for the individual with autism is going to be trial and error. Start with activities that the person in charge is willing to give a try. Be patient. At first you may just be able to include

49

the individual with autism in the practice of an activity, then expand to more responsible roles. In order for the person with autism to be included, the group needs to feel successful with the individual in it. In order to be competitive in a sport, or an activity where the whole group is being judged, the individual with autism may need to practice twice as much in order to succeed.

When you first start a new activity, you need to reward the small accomplishments that he makes. Each incremental improvement may equate to leaps and bounds. Other participants will join in the excitement if they see you rewarding these small signs of progress.

Try and catch the teammates doing something to support the individual with autism. Show them how to support the person and encourage him. The peers, coaches and teachers need the positive reinforcement for interacting, as much as the individual with autism does.

You may find that the individual with autism gets upset or angry when you try a new activity. Once he understands what is expected of him, you may find that he absolutely loves it.

This may take some time. Find out if the tears are just there to let you know that "this is hard" or if he has no interest in the activity. You may encounter this reaction with every new situation you try. This should not stop you from introducing new skills or activities. Initially you may shorten the duration and gradually increase the amount of time of the activity.

All the activities such as school plays, concerts, marching band

and sports may help him come out of the autism shell and join his peers. The excitement of being part of something special may help him deal with his fears.

Defining success as an incremental improvement will help you and the person you are helping feel successful. What may seem like a small accomplishment can lead to forward leaps on the autism spectrum

What may seem like a small accomplishment can lead to forward leaps on the autism spectrum.

Inclusion in Family and Special Events

Whether relatives or friends for most of your life, there is no guarantee people will understand you, your child, or the difficulties of raising a child with autism. As you are learning about autism you are also becoming the most knowledgeable person about the topic. You have an opportunity to teach those around you how best to interact with your child so that your child is accepted, and cherished by those you care about.

You will have many opportunities to teach your child social skills and appropriate behavior during the family gatherings and social events with your family and friends.

Depending on the type of event you are attending, you may choose to work on the generalization of skills you taught at home. As you are asking others to be understanding of your child's difficulties, you will also need to be respectful of their needs. A wedding ceremony is not the best place to start teaching a new skill. Places of worship often have spots next to the exit so that you can quickly remove yourself and your child from the facility if a tantrum is about to happen.

You may want to practice at the facility and bring lots of reinforcers with you for a test run. You can practice during events that

51

do not require total silence from the audience. Family gatherings

may be difficult at first, especially until the disruptive behaviors are under control. The gatherings tend to be chaotic, with new people, new environments filled with long waits and lack of structure. The child may not understand what is expected of him. What's important, however, is that you continue to follow through with the intervention you established at home and/or school if you can. This will help bring consistency to his life. Here are some suggestions:

- You may want to bring an activity with you that he likes to do while he is attending a family event.

- Initiate activities and games that your child is able to participate in.

- Share the responsibility with your partner. Bringing someone with you who can help take turns engaging your child with family and friends will make the event more enjoyable for you, your friends and family.

- Praise and reward others who take their time to interact with your child.

You will not be successful 100% of the time. Don't beat yourself up. You will have good and bad days, and so will your child. What is important is that you keep trying. You have a big job ahead of yourself: **You have to teach your child how to interact with the world around him and you have to teach the world around him how to interact with your child.**

Some of your relatives and friends will be very supportive, while others may have difficulty understanding. You can't win them all, but you have nothing to lose by trying. You'll find many true friends in the process.

Inclusion in the Community

The community wants to help. You will meet a few individuals who are not able to help you, but there are many others who will.

Just as at school, you can teach the child to learn and practice a task at home first. Once the skills are mastered at home, bring them out into the community.

Advance preparation may be helpful for the community members, prior to introducing the individual. Here are some examples:

- "Would you mind if my daughter asks you a question?"
- "Would you mind if she practices her conversation?"
- "Hi, my daughter is learning how to count out her money. Would you mind if we take a little extra time to do it?"

Do it only if they are not busy with other customers. **Black Friday is not a good day to do this!**

At first, you may find it hard to do. You may feel embarrassed and feel like you are disrupting their day. Practice makes it perfect, for you as well! With time, you will not even think about it. You will be so focused on making sure that your child or student is able to function in the community that the other feelings will disappear.

Search out the best places to practice the specific skills your child is currently learning; for example,

53

at stores, local businesses, restaurants, library, doctors office, etc.

If you find that business people there will not give your child a few minutes of their time, even though they are not busy, take your money to a business that will. Why would you support this kind of business in your community?

Throughout this book we have discussed children and students. This is because we tried to make this a tool for both parents and teachers. These techniques are not different for adults. What does change for adults is the extent of what the peers and community will find acceptable and appropriate behavior.

As the children with autism become adults with autism, they become more difficult to control. While they are young you are able to pick them up and redirect them. Once they are adults, some will be strong enough to pick you up and redirect you.

That's why it is so important to make every effort to get behaviors under control and to teach as many language and communication skills as possible. The same techniques that were used for teaching writing and coloring can be used to teach job skills and social skills. Whether the individual with autism grows up to live in a group home or is able to live independently, she will need to learn how to communicate and interact with others.

The educational system stops for many of these individuals once they reach age twenty-one. Public education may end but that does not mean that learning must stop.

Learning is a lifelong activity.

Every new word they learn, every new concept they understand, will make their lives easier and their future more rewarding.

54

Teacher's Role

There are several techniques a teacher can use in her classroom to aid a student with autism. If minor

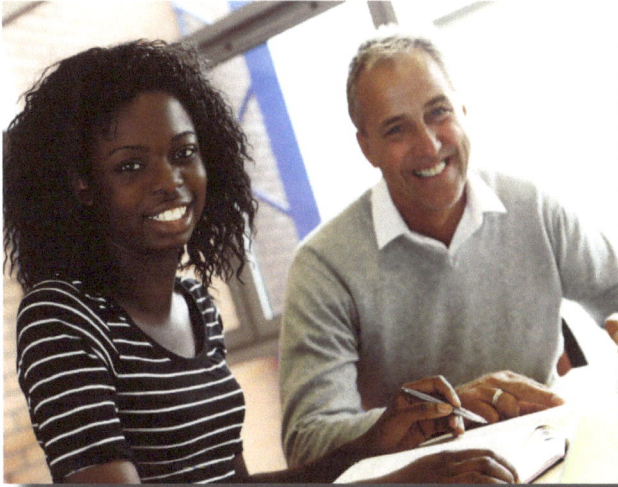

inappropriate behavior occurs, it is often best to ignore it since bringing attention to it may increase its frequency. Nevertheless, more disruptive behaviors such as talking aloud need to be corrected, as in the case of any student. Peer redirection is often the best way to get a student with autism back on task, but physical redirection may be necessary from time to time. In most cases, modeling the correct behavior via another student ("Watch Jamie do it,") or praising the student when the desired behavior occurs will result in a positive outcome.

Remember—when the student with autism is slightly off track, a subtle gesture (pointing) or prompt will often correct the problem.

Another important role for the teacher is to include the student with autism as much as possible in the classroom activities. Because they work so hard on behavioral issues and because of their difficulties in initiating conversation, the person with autism may be the best behaved student in a classroom. It is easy to overlook the quiet ones in the class, especially if the teacher gets some strange answers to her questions. It's easy to feel discouraged from involving the individual with autism since the teacher may get no response at all.

55

Since autism by nature is a socially isolating condition, peers can make a great difference in the progress of a student with autism. Most importantly, other students often serve as models of age appropriate behavior. Teachers can and should recognize peer interaction with the student with autism. They can initiate conversation. Students can provide critical intervention when a classmate with autism is lost in his schoolwork or needs redirection. A peer as tutor is perhaps one of the least restrictive ways for a student with autism to receive monitoring and guidance when only a little help is necessary. In coordination with the classroom teacher and case manager, it is also an effective means of cultivating responsibility and understanding of those who have special needs.

Younger peers may need to understand that autism is not something they can catch like a cold.

The teachers are an important resource for the peers. Younger peers may need to understand that the disorder is not something they can catch like a cold. Older peers may

have other fears or questions that the teacher might need to answer.

They may want to know what they can do to help out or need encouragement and recognition when they do. Statistics indicate that at some time in their career, teachers will encounter at least one student who, in the future, will be a parent of an individual with autism.

Staff Role

The administrative staff can make a world of difference for a student with autism. Lack of social awareness may present a student with autism in an unsafe situation. The more staff members are aware, the more everyone can be on the lookout for possible dangerous situations. Preventive measures need to be taken by the staff to ensure everyone's safety.

Training of teachers, peers and staff members will help everyone create a better school experience for the student with autism. Positive reinforcement works effectively to ensure those assisting the student are recognized as well. Everyone enjoys recognition for effort.

Raising awareness and tolerance for students with differences is an ongoing role that any administrative staff can fulfill. Autism presents the same challenge to educational professionals.

School Liaison or Behavior Specialist

The school liaison is the person assigned to supervise the welfare and education of a student with autism in the school environment. The school liaison may be a therapist who has worked closely with a student with autism in the home or specialized classroom.

He or she will usually sit in close proximity in the classroom initially and then, as the student with autism progresses, will sit farther away in what is called a "fading" procedure. This helps the student with autism gain independence and establish his own place in the classroom. This first phase may take months or even years, depending on the student's needs.

The primary objective is to have behavior stabilized so that learning can occur. As the school liaison assesses the progress of the student with autism, he or she will begin to monitor from a greater distance and with less direct intervention.

At this point, the classroom teacher, in consultation with the case manager, will be assuming a more natural role of teacher to the student with autism. When the school liaison is finally able to leave the classroom, the teacher should be completely in control and comfortable with the process of integration. Above all, it is the role of the school liaison to create a stable classroom situation for the teacher, student and peers of the student with autism before total independence in school takes place.

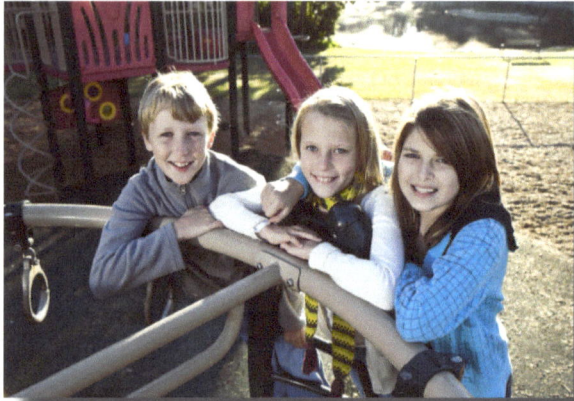

Peers

The peers are not trained therapists. Their goal is their own growth and education first. But there are opportunities where they can greatly contribute to the education of a child with autism.

A typical child can model how to behave or how to perform activities without direct interaction. Many peers volunteer to help a child with autism. These children also learn new skills themselves from the interaction.

They gain self confidence and a feeling of accomplishment when they see their friend succeed by their actions. Some may go on to careers as helping professionals.

Parents

The most important aspect for a parent is to understand how the interventions work. There are many opportunities for implementing them at home or in activities that are outside of the school environment. **Parents know their children the best. They spend the most time with them.** A parent will be a translator between their child and the world outside the school. In a lot of situations parents will need to fill in

58

all the roles since a lot of time they are on their own.

The more basic skills the parent possesses the more the child's learning can take place throughout the sixteen waking hours. **School makes up less than 20% of a student's waking hours.** Typical children continue learning outside of school, so can the child with autism.

Another way that parents can assist the child is with her appearance and hygiene. Children on the spectrum will not at first be aware of how their appearance impacts their social life. The more the child is dressed like her peers with a clean and organized appearance, the more approachable she will be to her peers.

Siblings

Siblings can be a wonderful resource in helping a child with autism. It is important to remember that they are children themselves. They may be dealing with the same emotions as parents when their sibling with autism acts up in public, yet they may not be old enough to understand it all. A sibling is a child, not a therapist. Although they may be a little older or even younger, they can help teach many skills. They can model skills, correct and reward, play games, etc. There may be times when they understand their sibling better than the adults. Helping teach their sibling may give them a way to interact with each other. Sometimes that may be the only opportunity for their interaction.

Katherine (Age 6) with her sister Bridget (Age 9) working on sight words.

Conclusion

Autism is a neurological disorder affecting about one and a half million Americans and their families. Psychological isolation and impaired social development are hallmarks of this puzzling condition. People with autism are often unable to process perceptions normally. They avoid eye contact, lack tone in their voice and facial expressions and at times seem unable to respond to others. Rituals, repeated motions and preoccupation with routines or details plague the individual with autism.

Although the above description of autism sounds bleak, much has been discovered in recent years that can ameliorate and even reverse the effects of this debilitating disorder. With early intervention, some children with autism develop normal patterns of behavior and language before they reach adulthood. Although these interventions require intensive, and at times exhausting work, research is now demonstrating their efficacy.

Although identified as a disorder by Leo Kanner in the 1940's, there is no known cure fo autism. Much has been discovered as to how an individual can learn and emerge as a participating member of the community. Many challenges will continue to face individuals with autism and their families. Along with the many challenges, there is now a great hope for those affected by Autism Spectrum Disorder. New techniques and educational methods promote greater interaction with the school and community. These techniques focus on preventing the social withdrawal which characterizes autism. Understanding, through education, is the first step in advancing the individual on the spectrum of autism.

Twenty years ago, it was highly unlikely for a student with autism to attend a regular classroom. As professionals in mainstream education became part of a team educating these students, progress has indeed taken place. It is remarkable what can be accomplished when parents, administration, teachers and peers and members of the community work together to include an individual as a participating member of society.

If "it takes a village to raise a child", it takes a city to raise a child with autism.

Thank you for being part of this lifetime effort.

Katherine in a marching band in competition.

When you first look at this information, you may think that it's only for professionals. I thought the same thing at first. I realize now how important these skills are for any parent of a child with autism. These skills are the basis of communication for you and your child. If you do not follow the same techniques in your child's daily routine, you may be undoing the work of others. By becoming a "parent-therapist" you may be able to multiply the gains your child can make.

Parents account for more than 80% of their children's learning time.

It is hard to act as a "therapist" when you see your child crying. You just want to hug her or make her feel better, but when she cries, she communicates with you. When you can remain calm and unemotional, you may be able to communicate with her by using your behavior. You are her main source of learning in the after school hours. School is only 30 hours per week. The remaining 82 of her waking hours is your opportunity to really teach and "reach" her.

If you learn the basic skills of teaching, prompting, and fading you'll be able to use them for the rest of your life with your child.

Therapists and teachers will come and go. With the knowledge of the teaching methods that work best for your child, you'll be able to assess who has the skills that are effective. As they come and go, you as a parent will be the only constant force through the years. The power of this force should not be underestimated.

You will be able to model these skills to your family members, your friends and community to show them what to do or how to act. It may be their first experience relating to someone with autism. There will be difficult and scary times. But there will also be plenty of joy to help you through. There is nothing more rewarding than seeing your child succeed as you work diligently and lovingly through each stage of challenge and growth.

You may contact Danuta: editor@katscafe.com.

Notes from Melissa

It has been my experience that the more we know, the more we realize there is so much more to learn. With every child comes a myriad of learning experiences and opportunities. Moving a person with autism on the spectrum of their abilities will help them succeed and lead to a more productive and independent life. This success hinges on a team consisting of parents, siblings, teachers and staff, students, peers and members of the community who are willing to work closely and communicate openly. Through a well-coordinated network of interaction involving the child and the greater community, growth can occur exponentially. It can also be inhibited by an unwillingness to try.

Not everyone will share your enthusiasm to help a person with autism. Some may be fearful of saying the wrong thing. Others may not know what to do or how to act. It may be their first experience relating to someone with autism. Nevertheless, there are very few who do not want to help. We all need encouragement. Continue to connect with others who care. Even a smile can make a difference!

Just as rainbow is a spectrum of colors , autism is a spectrum of abilities. Some are more colorful or vivid than others. Make life for a person with autism the most colorful you possibly can... get involved.

You may contact Melissa Niemann at: mn@niemannprofessionals.org

Moments - That Last a Lifetime

1995 (Age 9) Katherine as Princess Leia with friends helping her enjoy a Halloween parade around the school.

1997 (Age 10) Katherine was able to participate in a class concert with the support of the children on stage and adults behind the curtain.

1999 (Age 13) Community Theater production of "Annie"- Katherine is waiting with other cast members to get on the stage. Theater presented a lot of opportunities for her to learn. Frequently, Katherine did not understand what was happening. However, she figured out what to do by performance time with lots of help from her co-stars.

2001 (Age 15) Melissa and Katherine at Katherine's eighth grade dance.

2001 (Age 15) Graduation from eighth grade. Katherine independently went to get her diploma.

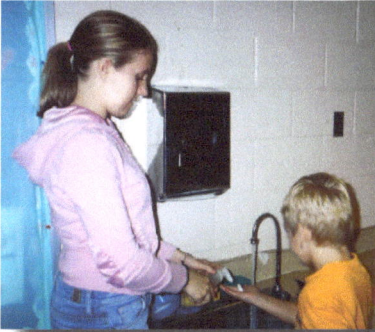

2006 (Age 20) Katherine is volunteering and helping children in a pre-school.

2007 (Age 21) Independently performing with the community college choir.

2009 (Age 23) Performing on classical harp for an art show. Katherine loves to share her music with others.

Every step is easier with a friend holding your hand.

References

1. Diagnostic and Statistical Manual of Mental Disorders DSM-IV-TR Fourth Edition by American Psychiatric Association (Jun 2000)

2. What is Autism? (March-April 2000, Vol. 33, No. 2) Advocate, The Newsletter of the Autism Society of America, page 3

3. http://www.cdc.gov/ncbddd/autism/hcp-dsm.html

Other Resources

If you would like more information go to:

http://www.niemannprofessionals.org

http://www.katscafe.com/autism_resources.html

www.autism-society.org

http://www.nimh.nih.gov/health/topics/autism-spectrum-disorders-pervasive-developmental-disorders/index.shtml

http://www.cdc.gov/ncbddd/autism/hcp-dsm.html

http://www.abainternational.org/

www.ingramcontent.com/pod-product-compliance
Lightning Source LLC
Chambersburg PA
CBHW041358090426
42741CB00001B/14